Essential Sight Words for Kids Learning to Write and Read

AF448081

this book belongs to :

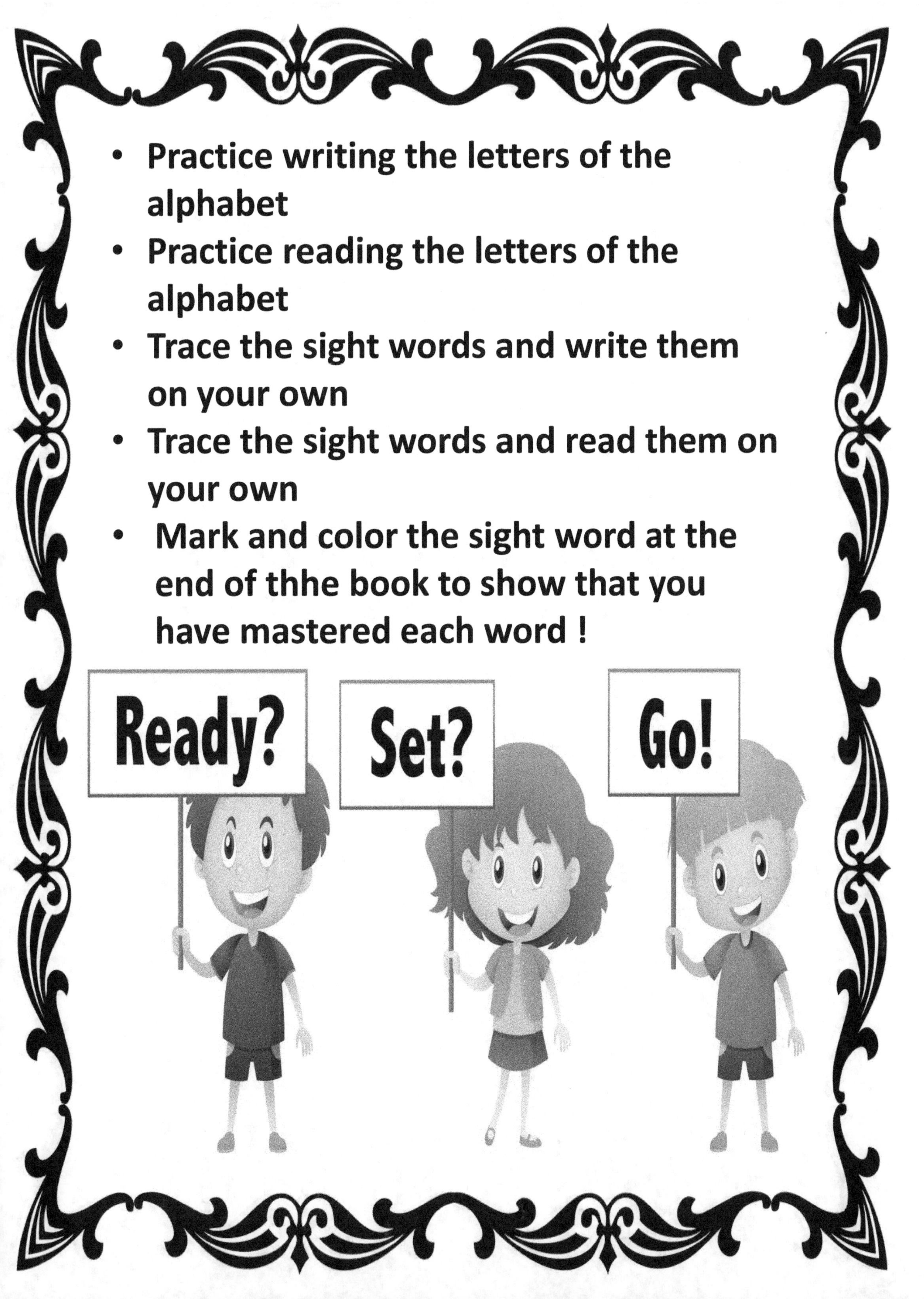

- Practice writing the letters of the alphabet
- Practice reading the letters of the alphabet
- Trace the sight words and write them on your own
- Trace the sight words and read them on your own
- Mark and color the sight word at the end of thhe book to show that you have mastered each word !

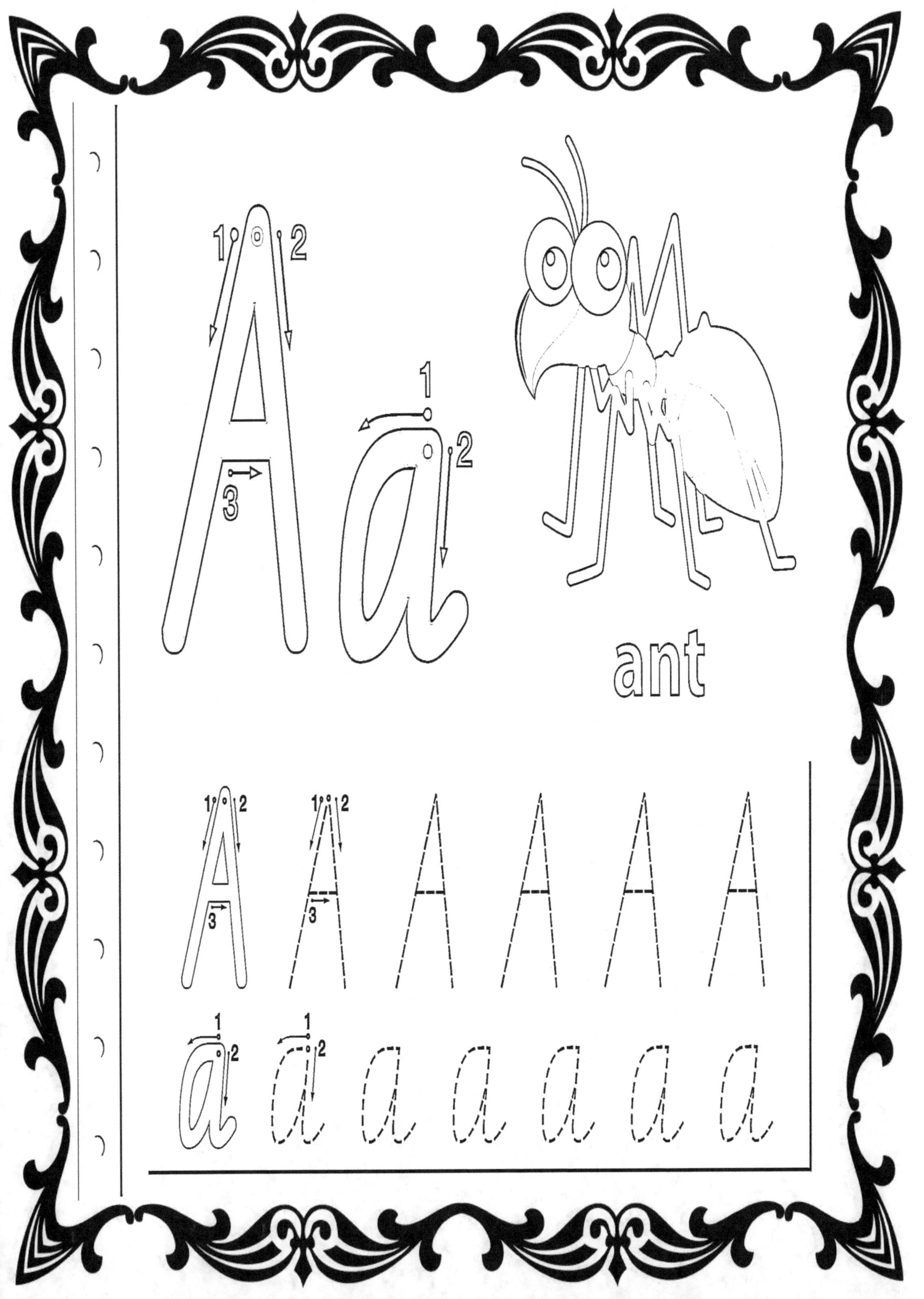

ant

Write the Letter B

Bicycle

Bicycle

Write the Letter C

Cow

dad

elephant

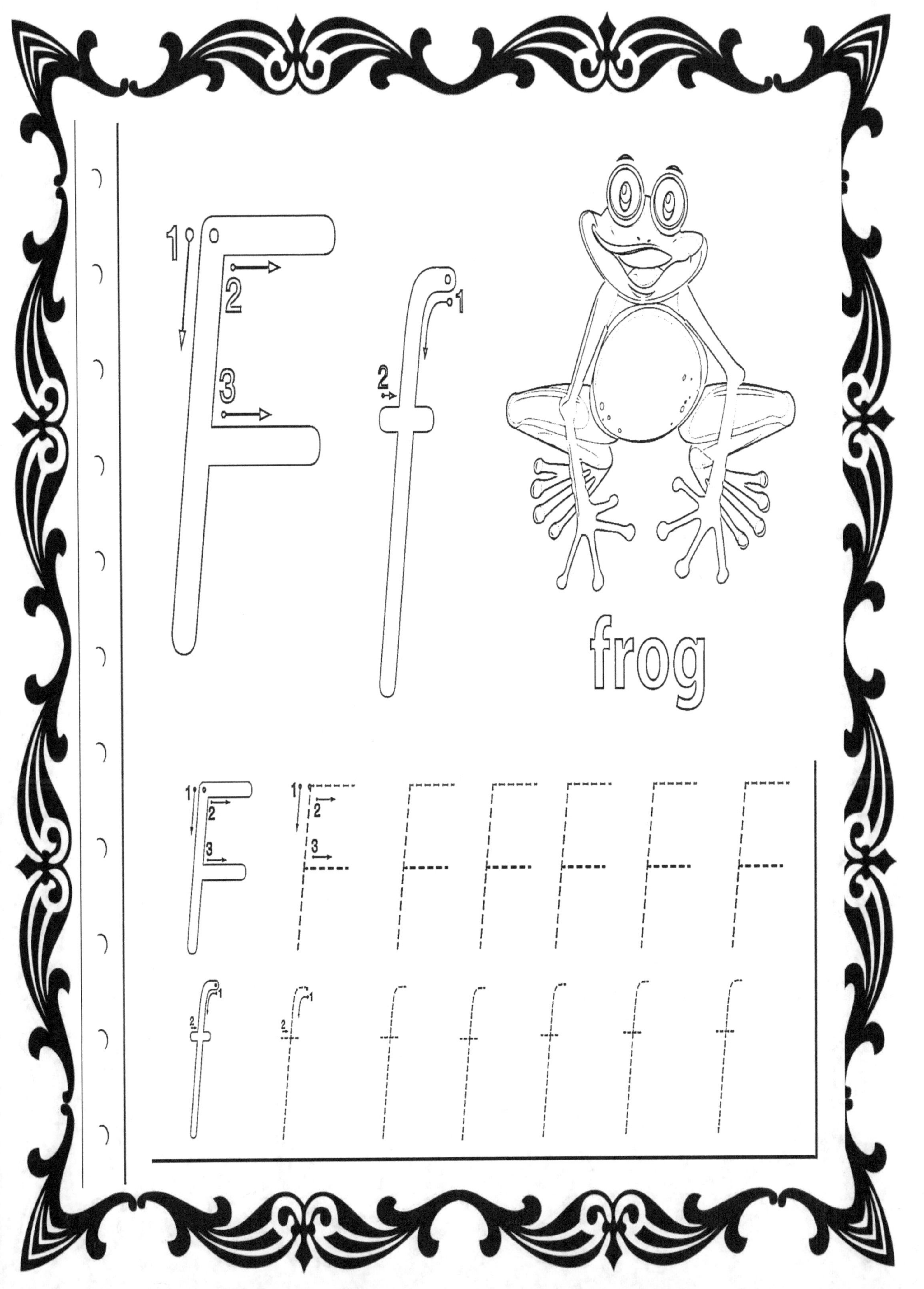
frog

grasshopper

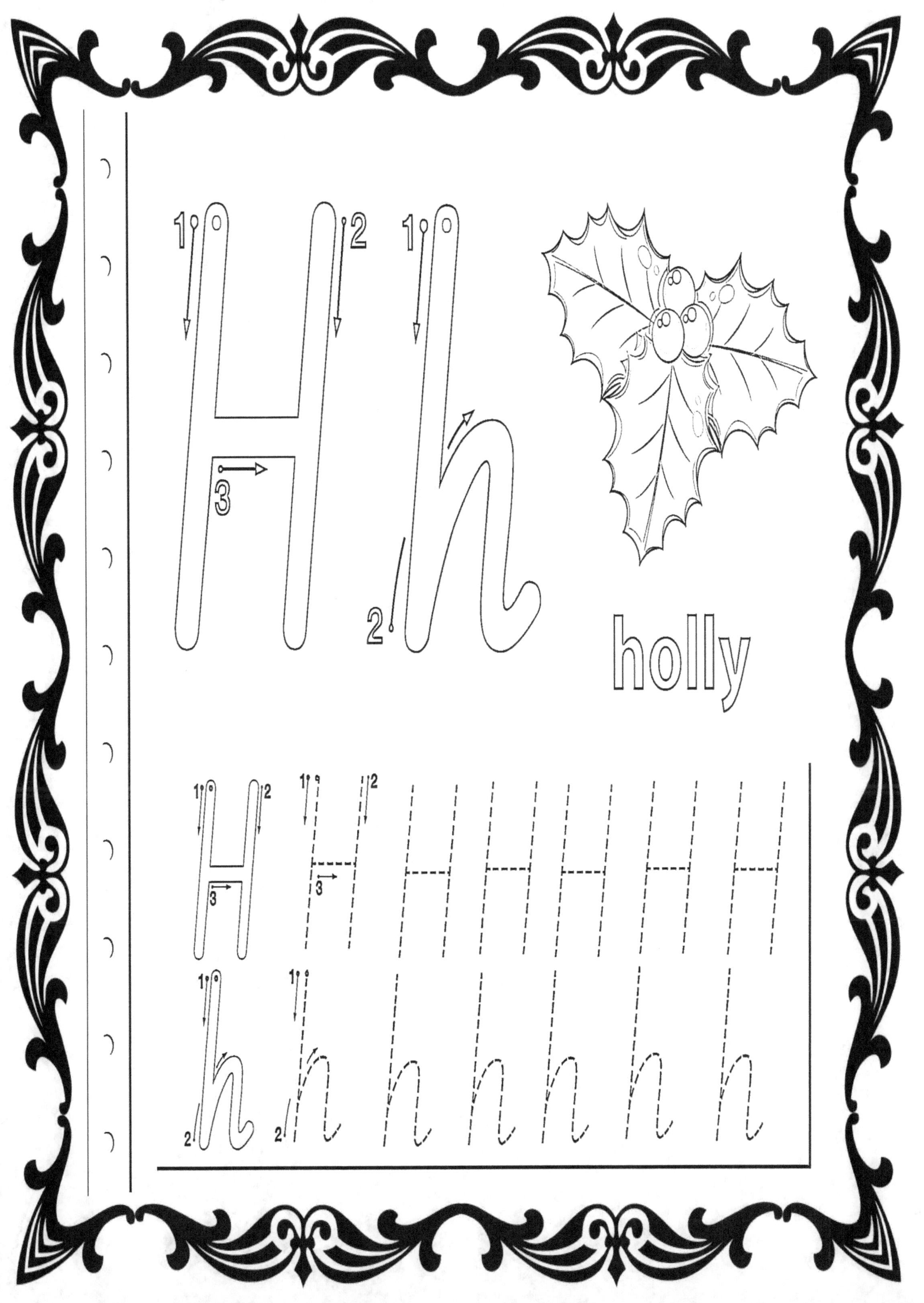

holly

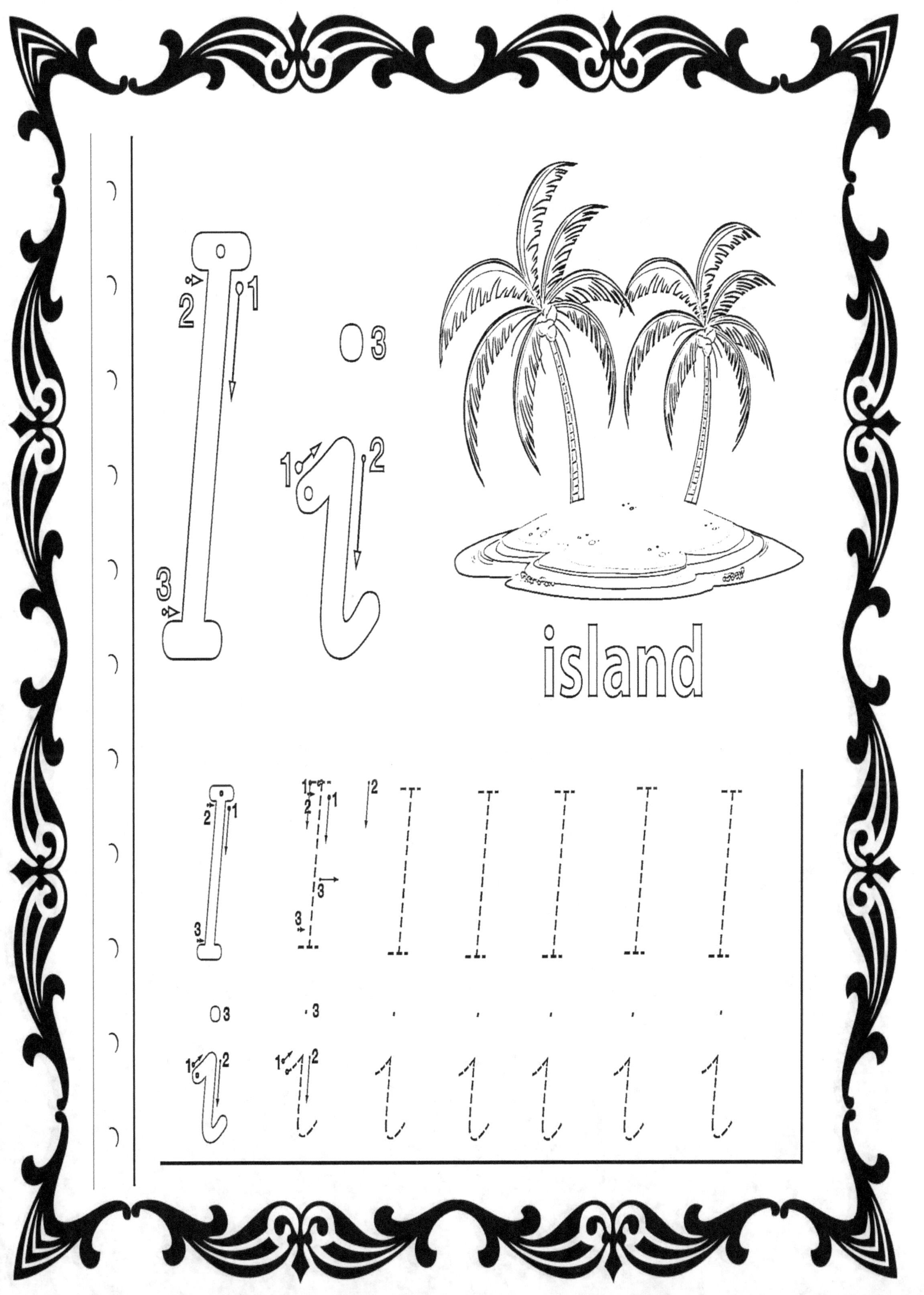

island

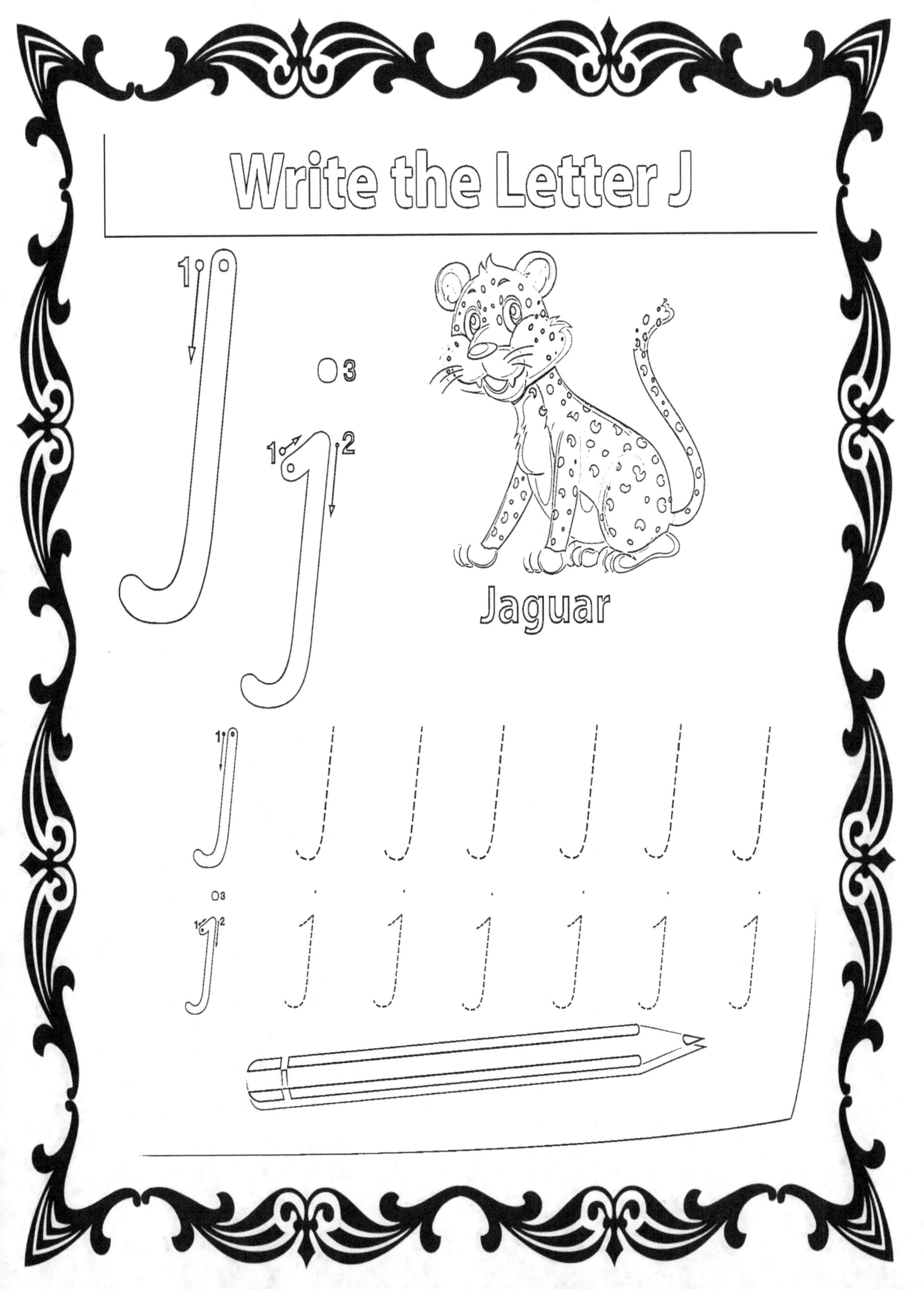

Write the Letter J

Jaguar

Write the Letter K

Kitten

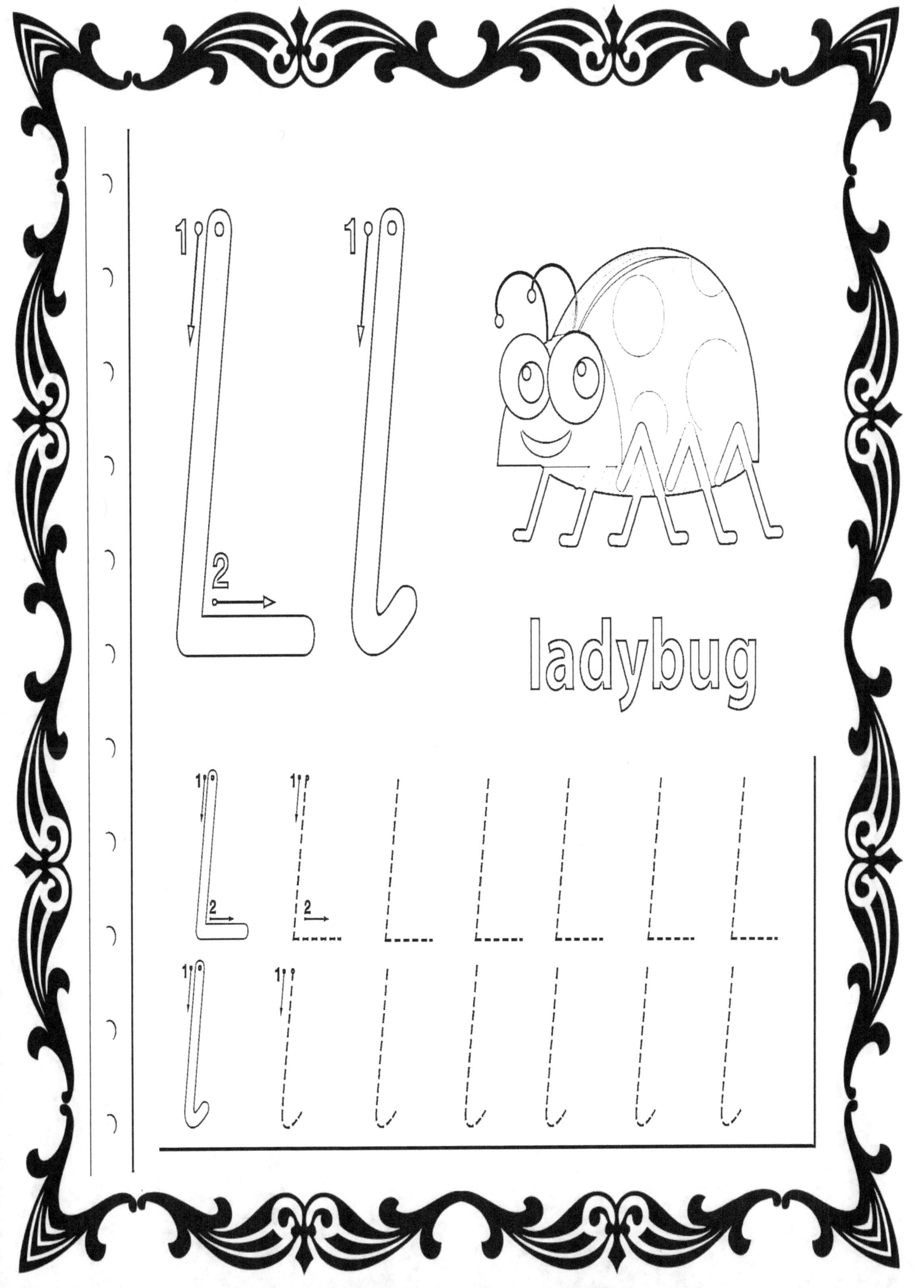

ladybug

moon

Write the Letter N

1
1
owl
1
1

pear

Write the Letter Q

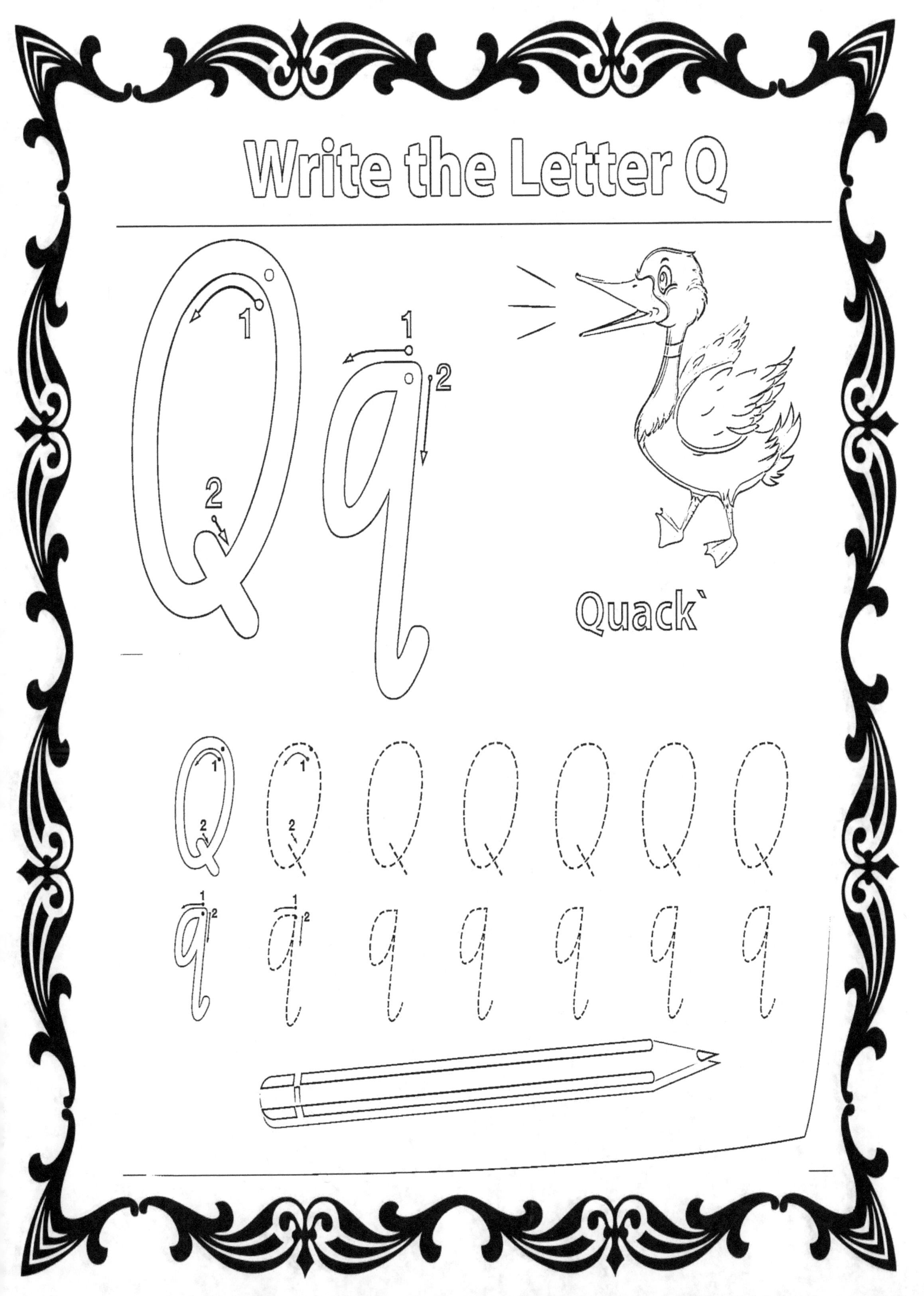

Write the Letter R

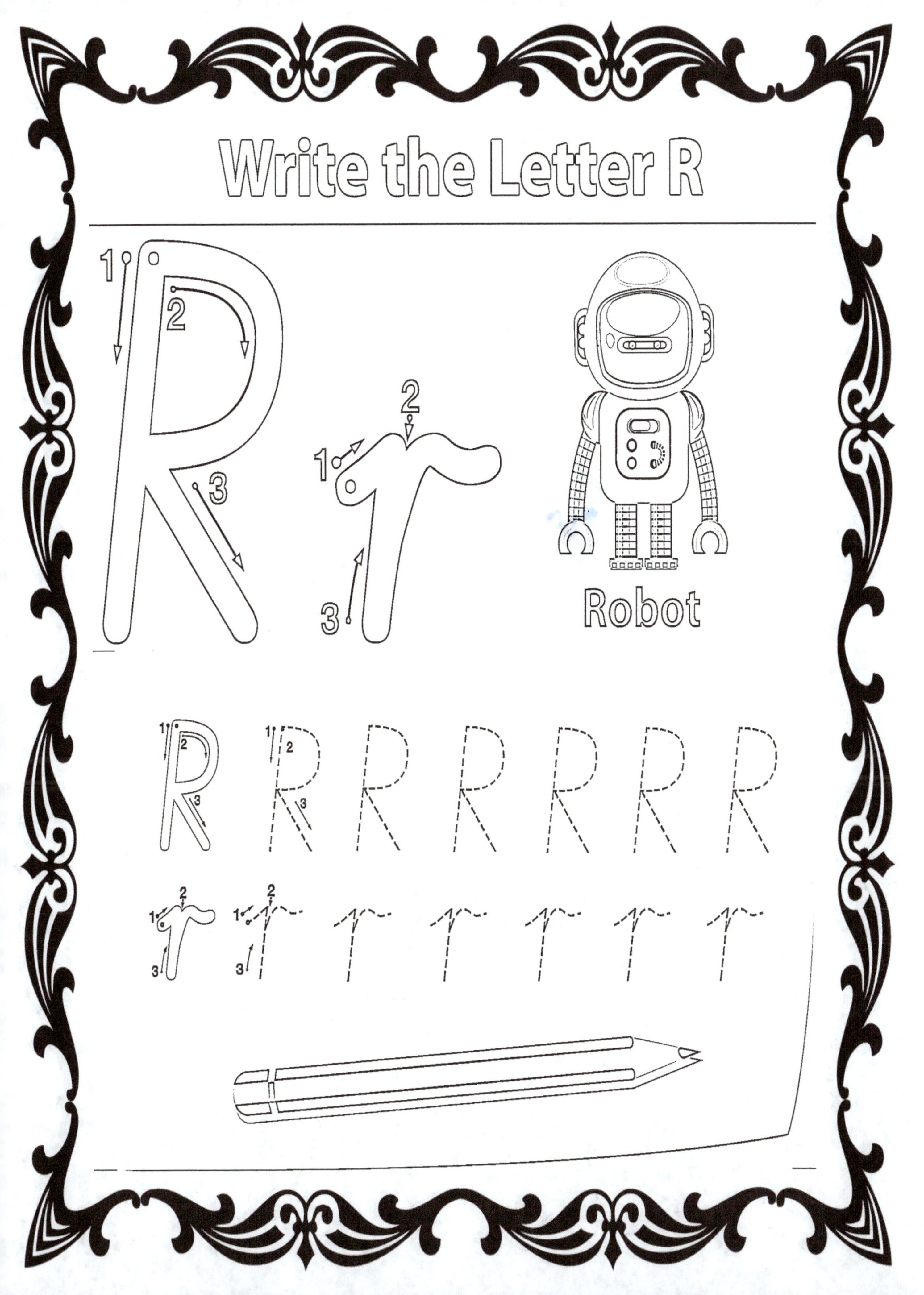

Write the Letter S

Snake

Write the Letter T

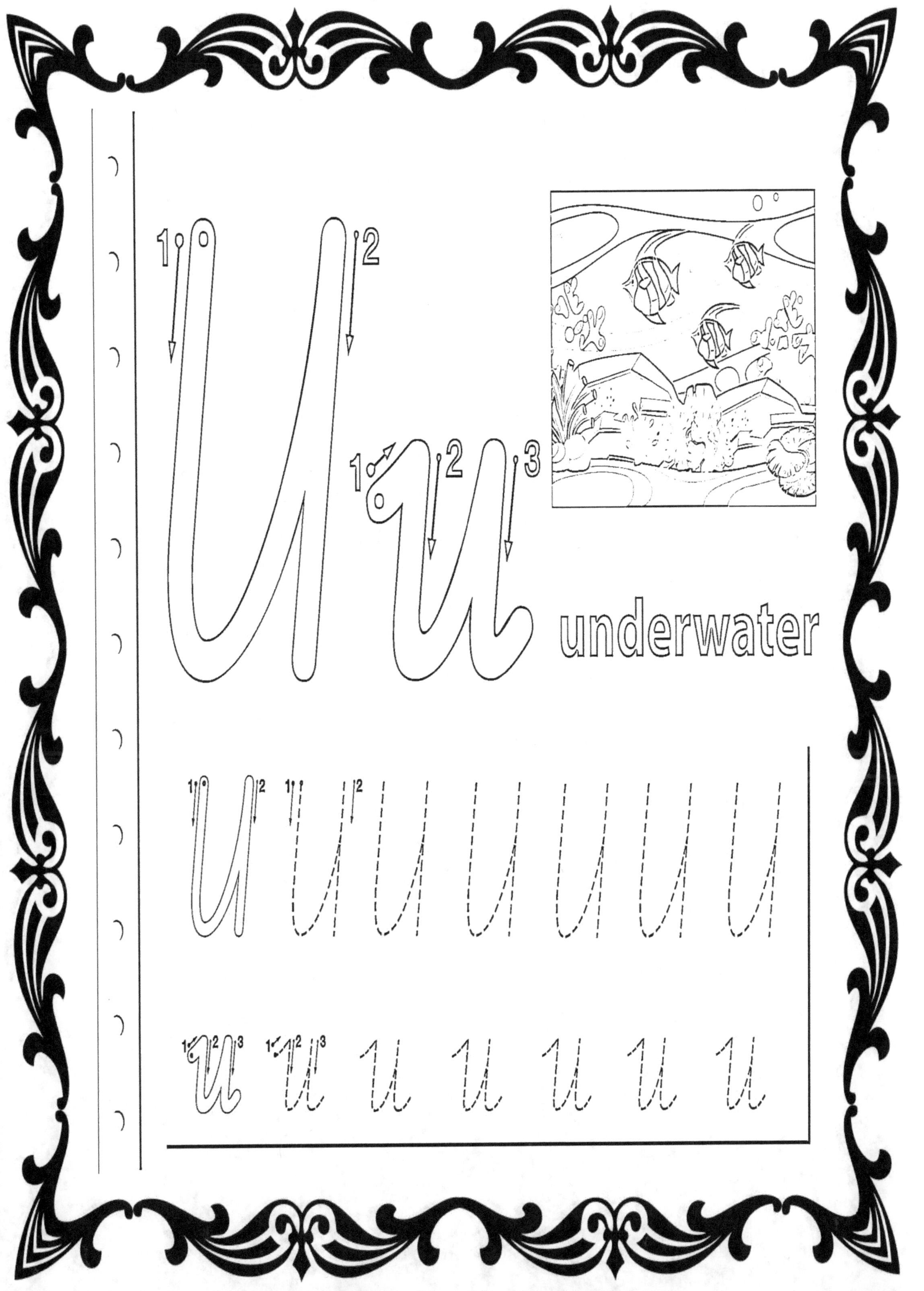

underwater

volcano

walrus

ALPHABET TRACING
WORKSHEET
Xx

ALPHABET TRACING
WORKSHEET
Yy
Yarn   Yo yo

ALPHABET TRACING
WORKSHEET
Z z

unicorn unicorn
vegetable vegetable
whale whale
xylophone xylophone
yarn yarn
Word Tracing
Trace the words that match each picture.

Word Tracing

Trace the words that match each picture.

apple apple
bird bird
cat cat
dog dog
elephant elephant
Word Tracing
Trace the words that match each picture.

koala koala
lion lion
monkey monkey
nest nest
octopus octopus
Word Tracing
Trace the words that match each picture.

Word Tracing
Trace the words that match each picture.

Write the letters Dd

Write the letters Ee

Write the letters Cc
Cc   Cc
_e ream
ro ket
hi ken

Write the letters Bb

Bb Bb

ear

vegeta le

ird

Write the letters Ee
E e
e e
e phant
monk y
tr

Write the letters Aa

B is for...
bed

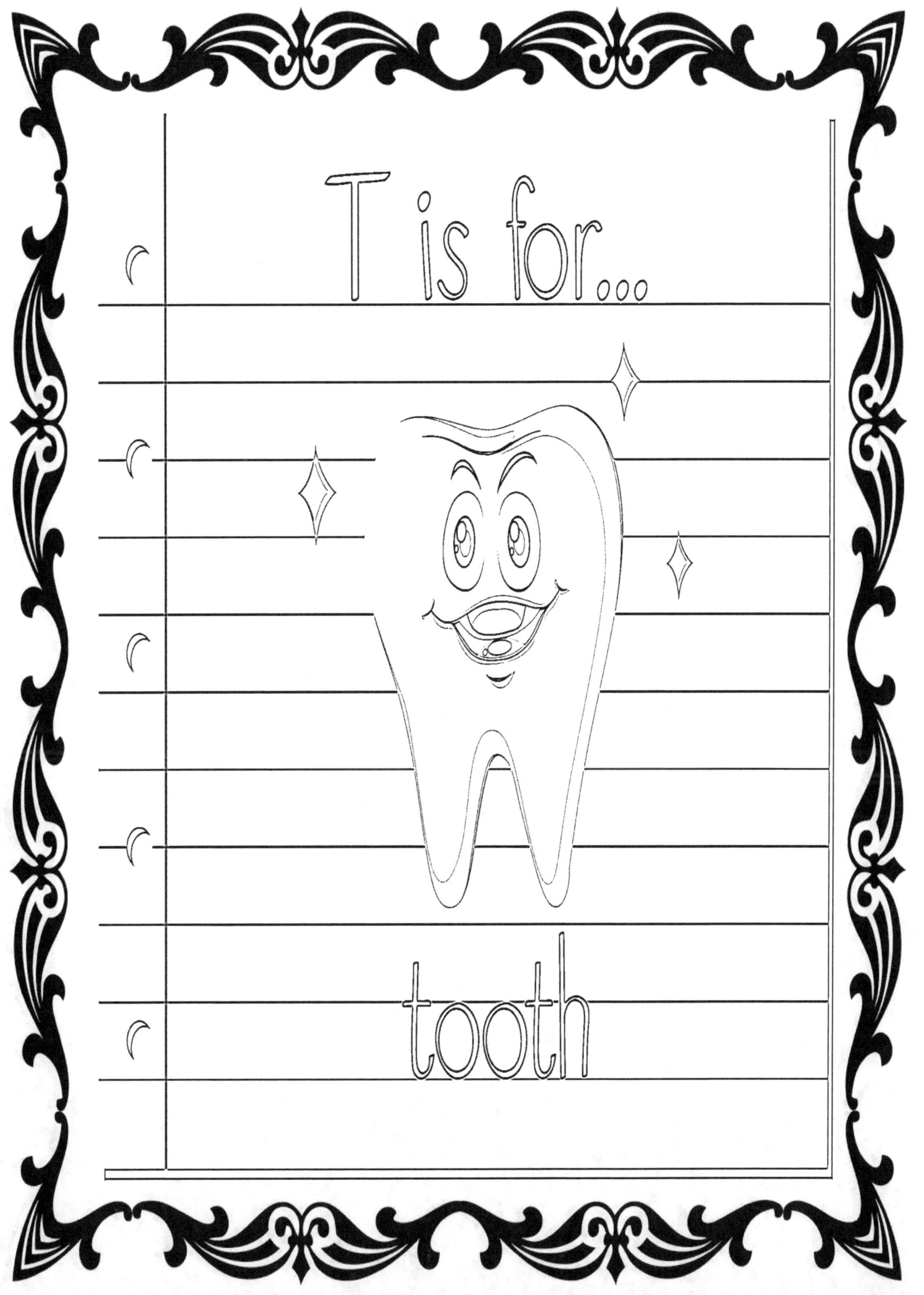

T is for...
tooth

W is for...
watering can

C is for...

chair

C is for...
clown

B is for...
boat

G is for...
Glue
glue

S is for...
soccer

L is for...
laugh
HA HA
HA
HA

C is for...
cave

T is for...
torch

J is for...
jellybeans

U is for...
underwater

I is for...
ink

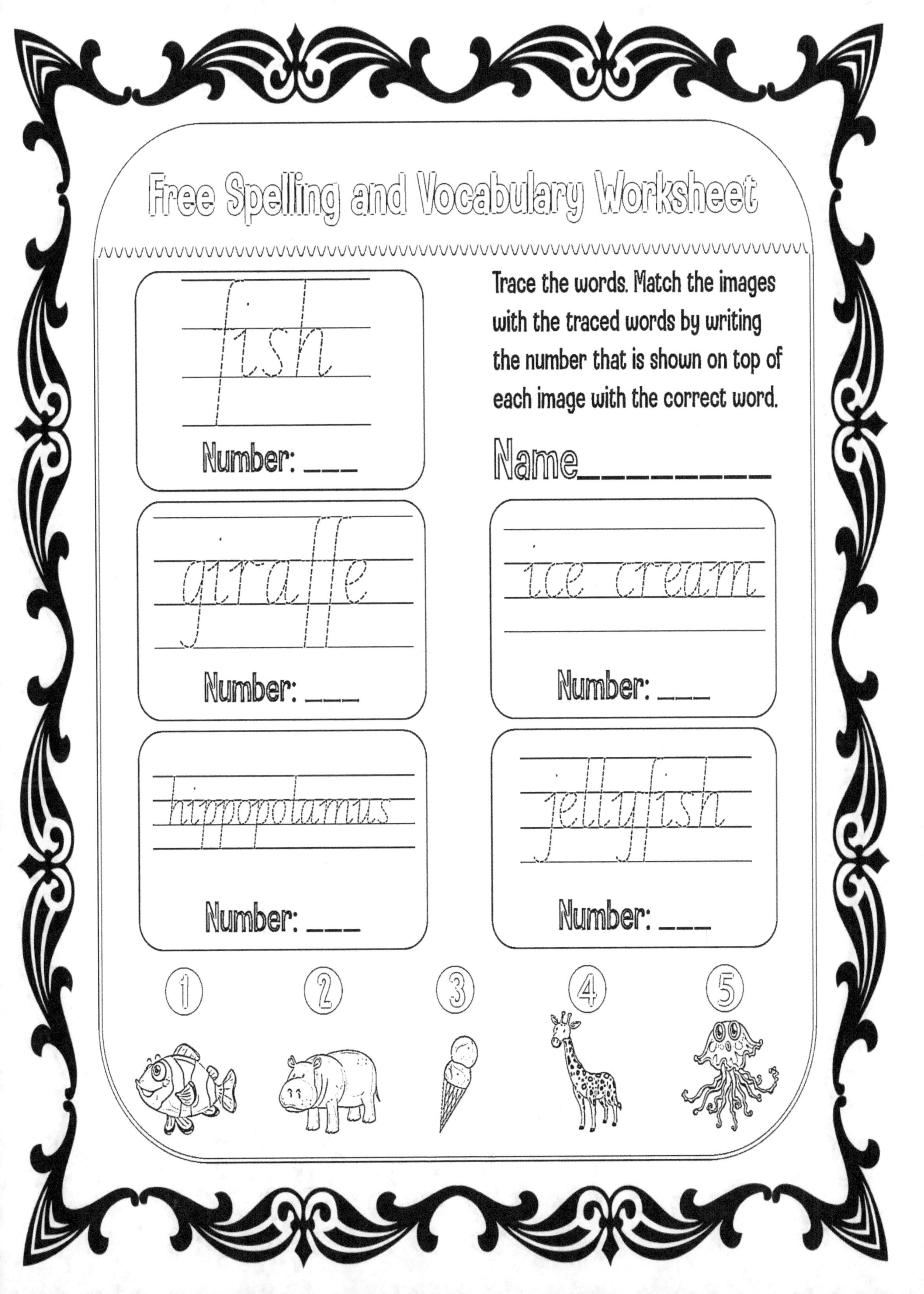

Free Spelling and Vocabulary Worksheet
fish
Number: ____
Trace the words. Match the images with the traced words by writing the number that is shown on top of each image with the correct word.
Name__________
giraffe
Number: ____
ice cream
Number: ____
hippopotamus
Number: ____
jellyfish
Number: ____
1
2
3
4
5

T is for...
treasure
tree
truck
tractor
trunk
traffic light
trees
tracks

T is for...
tapir
taxi
three
twister
tiger
teamwork
trombone
trunk

T is for...
tiger
table
Tasmanian tiger
teamwork
tadpole
tapir
toilet
taxi

T is for...
target
talking
tail
team
tarsier
tambourine
teaching
tiger shark

www.ingramcontent.com/pod-product-compliance
Lightning Source LLC
Chambersburg PA
CBHW081914120726
47996CB00010B/3315